Downside Up

A POETIC DISSERTATION OF THE DEHUMANIZATION OF AMERICAN CITIZENS

MARILYN MINETTE

DEDICATION

To you and me,
Our fathers, mothers,
And our ancestors.
The common men and women,
Who built America.
God bless us all!

Contents

ACKNOWLEDGMENTS

I withhold my thanks to everyone and everything that
contributed to this past couple of years, when hate took
control like never before…and a suspect disease became a
suspect criminal. Division, dissent, disgust, and
delusion…I withhold my thanks from all.

And though we live these troubled times,
I will forever be thankful that I was born
in the greatest country on Earth.

To her, I pledge my allegiance.
She will never fall.
God bless the United States of America.

JUST IN CASE

If you didn't read the prior acknowledgment, I believe it
holds meaning to the collection of these pages.
It reads as follows:

I withhold my thanks to everyone and everything that
contributed to this past couple of years, when hate took
control like never before…and a suspect disease became a
suspect criminal. Division, dissent, disgust, and
delusion…I withhold my thanks from all.

And though we live in troubled times,
I will forever be thankful that I was born
in the greatest country on Earth.

To her, I pledge my allegiance.
She will never fall.
God bless the United States of America.

PERSONAL

Take it personally, or maybe not.
Open your mind, expand a thought.
Don't take a side, simply stir the pot.
Nobody fits in one narrow slot.

Accept. Reject. Disagree. Agree.
It's not you. It's not me.
Opinion. Emotion. Frustration. Devotion.
Who do you really want to be?

If your life,
Is upside down,
Downside-up it,
All around.

POLITICO

I wake up slow,
Mirage days ago,
With a warm echo.
But now I must go.

I try to hold on,
Soon reality's gone,
Bittersweet dawn,
Brings with it the con,
Of white is black,
(Though white's still white),
And light is dark,
(Though light's still light).

How can that be,
That they tell me,
Just believe cra-zy,
Don't worry 'bout free?

How can that be,
An innocent plea,
Is met so angry,
Refuse to hear me?

How can that be?

My eyes can't see,
That open is closed,
Hey, money is free,
To all who agree.

'Now think like me,
And follow my lead,
I promise it's easy,
Just…trust…me.'

One thing is key,
It kills the psy-che.

I want to believe,
The plan is for better,
But lo-gi-cal-ly,
Everything's lesser.

I need to stand up,
I need to be heard,
They call me insane,
Not hearing my word.

Sense is not common,
No longer begotten,
Reality's clear,
The opposite's here.

Black is not white…
And dark is not light!
Up is not down…
So stop with the lie!

Close is not far,
A plane's not a car,
A thief's not a victim,
A pawn's not a czar.

DOWNSIDE UP

From suits in high places,
Masks and no faces,
You say open's closed,
And freedom's in cages.

I pray understanding,
I travel their mazes,
I try to assure them,
That jacks are not aces.

Still disillusioned,
I try hard to sleep,
I beacon the memory,
I pray my soul keeps.

My hope of all hope,
Of mere days ago,
I try to forget,
The lies I've been told.

I almost give in,
I calm deep inside,
And pray that I win,
To realize their lies.

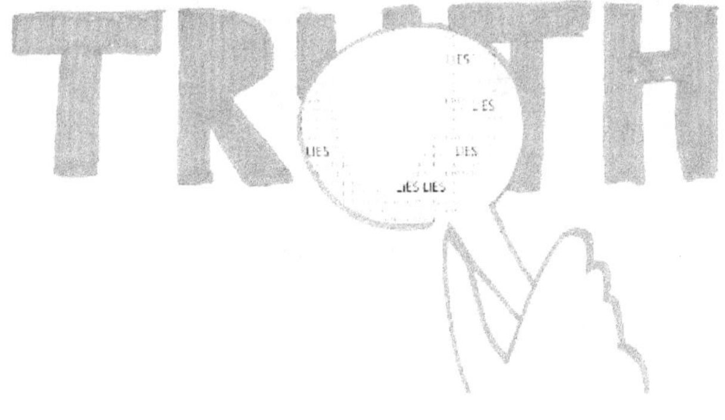

NINETEEN HUNDRED AND SEVENTY-FOUR

In nineteen hundred and seventy-four,
I sat in a class and smirked at the war,
Of words and deeds that sow the seeds,
Of things he claimed dehumanized me.

Watch out, be wary of laws that carry,
A false intent.
A fool's torment.

For long before you realize,
Your freedom waves,
Its last goodbyes.

And so it goes the wise man told,
Even a country,
Can be sold.

Secrets hid here,
Lies sold as cheer,
Thieves peddling fear,
Will summon an ear.

And one day you'll see,
Their vile hypocrisy,
Will dictate with glee,
Dehumanize me.

HARRY AND SALLY

You care too much what people think?
You've gone and bought the lie.
Live your life without the fear,
Of doom you're going to die.

Outlast the hype,
It falls to truth,
It knows no common sense.
You think you've lost,
Yet still persist,
The dope has no defense.

You will outlive the half of life,
Of propaganda lies.
Recall it can't survive the truth,
Irrational. Don't buy.

Calm the storm,
Reclaim the stable.
See the one across the table.
And when the question comes in passing,
Smile and say: "I'll have what she's having".

QUIET CRISIS

Know it or not, you're fighting a war.
You and your neighbor are against or for.
A culture born metamorphosis,
Capitalism, Christianity, Constitution crisis.

Don't laugh it's true,
Soon or late, it'll be you.
A jab, a job, one joke and done,
Will steal your life in more ways than one.

So if you're not wise, up it now.
It all depends on who and how.
The quiet crisis in silence descends,
What will you give to see it end?

TRAGEDY

They woke.
And pushed it far too far.
They broke.
And peaked beyond the bar,
Of reason, sense, intelligence.

Their tragedy.
Their final end,
They woke, they broke,
The joke's on them.

PRONOUNS

I'm proud to be all girl – her – she.
And he's so glad that he's a he.
It's nature, natural to be.
Exactly what we are.

You live in yours,
I live in mine.
And if we cross,
Always be kind.

Don't learn the hate,
They need to make,
You sing the loudest song,
For what you know is wrong.

Turn your back and walk away.
Don't let their words be what you say.
Just reach for him, and him for she,
Live your life and happy be.

For him or he or it or she,
For they or us or them or we,
Just live, let live our troubles free,
And be the who you want to be.

ENEMY OF THE PEOPLE

Guilt me. Shame me.
Silence. Blame me.
Dictate. Rule me.
Full-on ridicule me.

Words to cruel me.
Push tomfoolery.
Damn me. Command me.
Strand and brand me.

Strip me. Blind me.
Pain. Unkind me.
Stalk me. Mock me.
Cancel. Block me.

Disagree.
Un-freedom me.

Criticize me.
Neutralize me.
Demoralize me.
Lobotomize me.

Some day. Some way.
There's hell's high pay,
You'll face the fee,
For dehumanizing me.

MEDIA MAYHEM

Blather buster, hurricane.
Help! Before I go insane.
One says one, and two another,
Bogus bombs, now run for cover!

Every word with fear they play,
You better listen and obey.
Freedom is the price you pay,
If you live another day.

So, is it true or just a clue?
That lies are healthy misconstrues,
Of media on common man?
While they laugh and talk the plan.

They don't know the false from true.
Their ethics absent overdue.

For you alone, can turn the tide,
Cut the mayhem, let it die.
I for one will turn it off,
Stop drinking from their poison trough.

A brighter day tomorrow see.
Won't let their words brainwash me.

I'M OKAY, YOU'RE OKAY

I'm okay, you're okay,
At least we all were yesterday.

The world of late, has caused debate,
And questioned yours and my estate.

Decisions are no longer mine,
I hate I'm seen as borderline.

Over days and over years,
I query now with tears and fears.

Things are down that should be up,
How full or empty is my cup?

I'm okay, you're okay?
The world says *no,* we're not today.

HIDE

Hide behind what you can't see.
The keyboard is your friend.

You're bolder surer of yourself.
Blatant and sometimes rude.
But you don't care.

You're warm and cozy in your soft, plush bed.
The lights are low and your power screen glows,
The righteous words your fingers just said,
Blew them away with the lovely malice you spew.
But that's okay, they don't know you.

You turn it off and close the lid,
Sink your head into your expensive pillow,
And hum.

And for a split second, you wonder.
Was that me?
Then immediately forget.
No accountability.

Hide behind a false bravado,
Erode your worth and self-esteem.
And the saddest part of all?
No one cares.

HOME

Yes, she's tattered, frayed, and torn,
Too often a spoil of misled scorn.
And yet most all that come remain,
And those that born to live lay claim.

A hopeful beacon light to heal!

Those in need,
All nations bleed,
The hurt of her demise.

But do not, never count her out,
Disparage her, unwise.
At last to glean sweet liberty,
Her purpose will abide.

PAYDAY

I didn't buy this, but I'm paying for it.
Scolded like a child,
As I toil to defend mine.
Speak ye the truth,
But don't make headlines.

I didn't buy this, but I'm paying for it.
Buy me a dollar with this worthless thin dime.

THE GREAT DIVIDE

I am not the judge of you,
But I can judge the things you do.
You are not the judge of me,
Cope with what we disagree.

Don't buy into the great divide,
It foils their plans of spoils and lies,
Here we go don't trust the flow,
Of information high and low.

Oil and water do not mix,
Much like pills and politics.
While they try to force our hand,
Recall our country, together we stand.

Make wrong right,
Not right wrong.
We both agree,
United we're strong.

BLIND EYES

Among the sheep,
There hides a fox.

Don't roam your eyes,
In useless talks.

For overnight,
His cloak of dark.

From inside out,
He eats your flock.

TWO WEEKS

I'll tell you now I'm gonna drink too much,
Go water down that wine.
Can't near escape, gone crazy nuts,
Early or later it costs your mind.

Wax-on-wax-off, just how I feel,
'Cept minus the sanity, cold nerves of steel.
How do they want me? What's today's news?
It's a bad comedy. Gives me the blues.

Two weeks turned years,
Still comes with fears.
Decisions are hard,
But I hold my own cards.

No more for me! Keep bending to strife?
Hell no, bye-bye, riddins, goin' back to my life!

SOCIAL-SUICIDE

We are our own worst enemy.
Self-destruction at its finest.
Lower your standards, you'll feel better.
More is fallible, better is lesser.

Stop complaining, things could be worse.
Friends and family see less than a year.
Stay away and lick your wound.
No one needs an unessential you.

MILLION-DOLLAR BUTTERFLIES*

Love the yellow butterflies,
Blue ones, black ones, fly so high.

They need no pain, experiments.
Don't even need the government.

So do they know it's raining riches?
Do they see the gold and glitches?

They don't care. Don't give a damn,
They laugh and glide without a plan.

You see, million-dollar butterflies,
Don't need you to live their lives.

*read the BBB bill

LETTERS

A B C D E F G,
Hello, tell me what you see.
H, I, J, K, L M N O P,
Tell me what you think of me.
Q, R, S…T, U, V,
What I say, do you agree?
W, X, and Y and Z,
Just live and let live happily.

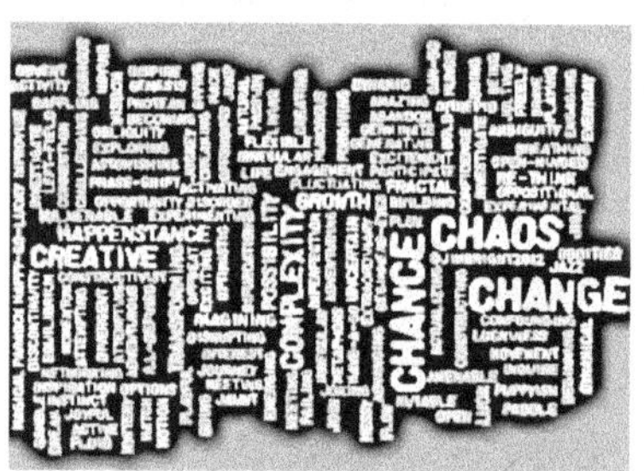

DESENSITIZE

My mother died,
I cried and cried,
Now years go by, I try to try.

I read a story,
He passed in glory,
Admirers praise his legacy.

A tragedy,
High casualty,
Their names stir something deep in me.

The evening news,
Bleak numbers grew,
And quick, another where, what, who?

The plague invades,
Our leaders say,
What no one cares about.

"While it makes us very sad,
A million's really not so bad.
A few more thousand every day,
Not a terrible price to pay."

I walked away,
Recalled the day,
The day my sweet mother died,
And now, I fear…I am desensitized.

GOVERNMENT GOD

It's me, not you,
To see me through.
My parents taught me well.

Family ties,
Friends don't tell lies.
No government god to tell.

Community is my family.

But mostly there is God,
Some think it odd.
No politics prod.

And when I look,
I do just fine.
A happy soul in me I find.

Thank you God, parents, family, and friends,
My wounds encountered, will surely mend.

WHO?

Say *ver, ve, xem, xe,*
Zir, ze, too.

The clouds bring clout,
To those left out.
Lest we forget,
The ones in doubt.

Say *e,* say *eir,*
Say *fae,* say *faer,*
And *per,* and *pers,* too.

It all brings tears,
To my searing ears,
And thoughts too lost,
Amongst the fears.

I stretch back and wonder.

Who did I omit?
I feel like such a twit,
But only split-a-moment,
Cause it's all bull shit.

BELIEVE

Do not believe,
What your pretty eyes see.
What your ear hears,
Or what your heart fears.

Enjoy Downside Up,
We're happy to fill your cup,
Nine-tenths of empty,
Is more than plenty.

Where everything's fine.
You won't need a dime.
Just pay with your soul,
Then relinquish control.

Our fictitious reality,
Is the best of inanity,
But no worries here,
We'll fuel all your fears,
Of everything mythical,
Physical, political.

So welcome to Downside,
Don't hope for the Up,
We're so glad you're here!
Now let's empty that cup.

MONEY MOUTH

Put your money in your mouth,
As you tell me what to do.
Let me see you walk your walk,
Before I follow you.

Sayin' it ain't makin' it,
Practice what you preach,
Lead by your example,
We know all talk is cheap.

Put not your trust in princes,
Their effort soon goes south,
So, when you lead or follow,
Put your money in your mouth.

ALIKE

If we were alike,
We couldn't celebrate diversity.

If we were alike,
We'd never have beautiful music,
Grand art,
Or quantum theories.

If we were alike,
We couldn't think beyond the known,
Or tempt beyond the unknown.

If we were alike,
We'd all die a dull death,
Of sameness, of blandness, malaise,
And ignorance.

And our lives would be worse.

THANKS TO COVID

Thanks to Covid,
We know friends and foes.
Our new metamorphosis,
Unconscious consciousness.
Directives and class.
Division amass.
Our place in society,
That's doled with anxiety.

Thanks to Covid,
We know what they're made of,
What they stand for,
And what they cave to.
And cave they do,
To the voice of a few,
Whose issues are skewed,
And truth is taboo.

Thanks to Covid,
Stream off the internet,
See our school's heart,
Our faculty's goal,
Hold parents apart.

Thanks to Covid,
Victims are bad guys,
And bad guys are victims.
Your struggle squeaks by,
As your witness tells lies.

Thanks to Covid.
Politics' sideshow.
'Follow the science',
Leaves nowhere to go.

Thanks to Covid,
This could last forever,
Wake up now take up now,
Your life,
Or it's never.

CAVE

Cave - /kāv/ - verb – to capitulate.

Example of using cave:

While disappointing leaders *cave* to false gods,
Good policy,
Common sense,
And doing the right thing,
Die tragic deaths.

FOOL'S GOLD

Soundless majority, apathy reigns,
A few loud voices, they're to blame.
Lull the muted, divide and cheat'em,
Silence is their death of freedom.

Forbid you be among the broken,
Think, my friend…silence is not golden.

CHOSEN

I know a girl in misery,
Whose life is mostly history.
She lives entrapped by words of fear,
Of last night's news with mourning tears.

Yet as she looks, the sun is bright,
She only sees her pity plight.
A free flight bird she used to be,
Now sits in chained mentality.

Unfortunate she's not alone,
She has a house but not a home.
To fly again her only wish,
Against all odds she must exist.

To heal regain stability,
Along with new integrity.
Example she the chosen one,
Will represent forgotten sons,
And daughters too,
Like those in lieu,
Of possibilities.

TERMINATOR

Protests here. Demonstrations there.
Always two sides to a story.
A rape. Incest.
An unwanted mess.

But most are lucky.
My body, my own.
My dream come true.

Boy meets girl. Could it be love?
Yes, indeed!
Can't you see?
We're happy as can be!

But now we're not so sure.
Just one of those things.
Don't call it 'with child'.
Let's not say 'going to have a baby'.

Already pushing away,
The truth you cannot say.
Block it all out,
At least for today.

Let's get a sign and join in.
Don't forget to pop the pill that'll end all your woes.
Now, they come in the mail, guilt free.
Swallow your troubles away.
My dream come true.

Let's hoist that sign,
Don't give it a mind.
Make your heart blind,
Leave feeling behind.

Don't think about it.
Just keep pushing it back.
A year, or two, or three, and twenty.

Look behind you.

What have you gained?
What have you lost?
Is your heart a bit troubled?
What was the cost?

Don't answer those questions,
They're all just taboo,
Only one really matters,
(Should have thought this through.)

Was Mother-like-Daughter,
Your dream come true?

If your answer is yes,
I must confess,
And clarify to you, you know…
Your life would be a big fat NO.

No breathing, or laughing, or smiling, or loving.
No playing, or sharing, or singing, or running.

Souls left unwanted.
Smiles eyes won't see.
Hands that won't touch.
A child just wants to be.

Gone forever.
Millions of never.
Brings anger and tears,
For lives lost years.

In ending I'll ask,
An honest pursue,
Of an alternate view...

What if your Mother,
Terminated you?

37

WHO'S A FOOL?

Remember, most leaders aren't stupid.
The outcome they realize is usually exactly what they want.

WORD TO HATE

Let's take a break and play a game,
One that just might push insane.
Sit back, relax, and have some fun,
All join in, both smart and dumb.

Give a trendy word you hate.
Me! I know one – mitigate!
They think it's cool, so smartly oozed,
Sophisticated class abused.
Went unused to overused,
Yes, mitigate shove it down the tubes!

Okay, that's great, now who is next?
Here, I've got one in a text.
The ever-undefinable woke,
Some even push it to a joke.
Used to be past tense of wake,
Adopted now extreme of fake.
Ideal of woke is good at core,
But humans gnarl to twisted gore.
Too bad we warp beyond extreme,
And lose ideas of true supreme.

Downside Up

Last call, a word of agitation?
No question. It's misinformation!
Has no true identification,
Censors lack accreditation.
Facebook, Twitter, Tic and Toc?
Youtube? Hell they got no doc.
Lies roam free, some truths are banned,
Money talks, it does not stand.
Politics, opinion spews,
Bunch of garbage in the news.
Chances are that if you listen,
Half what you hear misinformation.

40

SOLUTION

Let's all cancel everyone!
You cancel me and I'll cancel you.
Then finally, we can get back to living our lives.

41

ANOTHER SOLUTION

Let's all get impeccably woke and live it for a day.
Then we'll realize the reality.

Fact: we're all human.
And in all my travels I've never met a perfect human.
Not even me.

THE FINAL SOLUTION

Look honesty in the face.
This our final key.
You know who you are,
Tell he who needs to be…

Shut your mouth long enough to listen to another's
opinion.
You'll learn something.

Open your mind.
Yours is not infallible.

Unlock your heart…
Or did you loose the key?

Seek compassion.
Not contempt.

Put hate away.
Embrace love and understanding.

You may need me one day.
Don't push me away.

Downside Up

No *one* has all the answers,
Not me, not you.

Sometimes your right,
But sometimes your wrong.

We're all in this together…
Lest we lose our way.

I pray we all choose wisely.

BELIEVE

Believe it or not,
We must, but not them.
Believe it or not,
We pay for their gin.

Believe it or not,
We trust as they lie,
Believe it or not,
They mock while we die.

Believe it or not,
Sell 'them' against 'us',
It's hard to believe,
In America don't trust.

A nation at odds,
As odds do odd ways.
Believe it or not,
They led us astray.

DON'T WAIT

Don't wait too late,
To debate the hate,
Don't overrate the underrate,
Of states with misled aggregates.

Of mandates and degenerates,
Of candidates and delegates.

Don't dictate the bait,
Of the fake and innate.

Elevate the great!

Celebrate first-rate!

Obliterate the fake!

Amputate deadweight!

But don't wait too late,
To start the debate.
Keep that date,
To set it all straight.

DE-HUMAN-THEE

The world sheds a tear,
For those that aren't here.
Who died early death,
Without a last breath.

Of great artists claim.
Great minds do the same.
Scientists lost.
Forever a shame.

Great leaders everywhere could be,
Maybe save lives of you and me.
Write great works of sanity,
To lead the world's humanity.

It's sad, so sad, so very sad,
On contemplation, makes one mad,
To think the first in human deaths,
Ranks number one is Mother's mess.

Rethink the man that could have been,
Our savior from the devil's den.
Imagine a she will never be,
The greatest dancer never see.

My body my choice I do agree!
Until a part becomes a 'me'.
So don't think once, think two or three.
Before you choose, de-human-Thee.

WHY ARE WE HERE?

Made in America.
The blue bird flies.
Good jobs for all.
Cheeseburger and fries.

The rich want war.
My daffodils bloom.
Actors pretend.
Music's perfume.

Policies mysteries.
In God I trust.
Silent no longer.
Live or bust.

SIMPLE MATH

A half truth equals a whole lie.

HELL ON EARTH

If you spew empty lies,
Play hookie from work,
Abandon what's right,
And do the absurd…

If you love to do nothing,
Cheer on the brawl,
Don't take a stand,
Life's hell for all.

TIRED AND SICK

Thirsty for a speck of fact,
Instead a piece of gossip?

Would you like to sip sensation?
Rub the shoulders of the rich?
Maybe get more compensation?
While you play the ruthless bitch?

Or are you tired and sick of tsars,
With lipstick on their face?

Tired and sick of those that think,
You're dumber than a rock…
Condescending, shame and gloom,
Expect the lesser, years of doom.

Here's a piece of good advice:
Don't look back and don't think twice,
Forge ahead and live your life,
Forget the fad, do what's right.

TEAM

I don't care if he-turns-she.
I don't judge, I just judge me.
But when a he beats all the shes,
Where all compete requires no he's.

Well, that's not right, ridiculously,
A female race with he-turned-she?
This is dumb stupidity.
Let me explain it basically.

A baby's born a he or she,
There is no more you must agree.
Now, if one decides to he-turn-she,
No flesh and bone will change bo-dy.

He-turns-she is still inside,
No matter how they try to hide,
He's still a boy like baby born,
In strength, endurance, testosterone.

The she's that train for years to show,
Their goal of perfect, share the blow,
When he-turned-she disrupts the flow,
To always cheat'em, push'em low.

Now I ask you, is that fair?
If this was you, wouldn't you care?
No longer does a team compare.
All she's defeat - that leads nowhere.

HISTORY

Let history repeat itself,
We haven't learned it yet.

Remember it, but don't look back,
Chase the crazy, fill the lack,
Of understand misunderstood.
What you couldn't and what you could.

Another year to change your fate,
Another day to set it straight.
Begin this minute right away,
Your better person starts today.

55

2019…2020…2021…?

Bow down,
To the absurdity of this moment.

A MOTHER

Take my time,
Take my money,
Change my mind,
With words of honey.

But when you fail,
And call the lies,
Don't cross the line,
Or someone dies.

I'll pay your taxes,
I'll bite my tongue,
Follow the rules,
Even take your shun.

But when I hear,
Your final lie,
You better hands off,
Or someone dies.

Don't cross the line,
Don't even try,
My child is mine,
For him I'll die.

For the last of time,
Once more I'll say,
Don't cross the line,
I promise you'll pay.

CRY WOLF

They don't know me,
But they said I'm to blame,
For what, they didn't tell.

They say it again.
Over again.

They said numbers are racist,
Roads are racist.
Engaging debate is racist.

They say it again.
Over again.

They say the flag is racist,
My favorite food is racist.
And trees are racist.
Even my unborn child.

They say it again.
And over again.

They say, just submit.
Turn off my heart,
Lobotomize me.
Cauterize me.

They say it again.
And over again.

Repeat your mantras.

Over again,
And over again,
Over and over,
And over again.

Say it forever,
Plus one more.
Fake aims won't kill,
In your one-sided war.

I'm looking at you,
Your words prove untrue.
They spill of *your* racism,
Everything ill.

Quiet and listen,
Hell's ringing its bell.
You don't believe them.
And I never will.

59

THE REAL NEWS

I installed a lie detecter app on my cell phone.

Now, all my news apps get slower and slower…
And often don't even connect.

Hmmm.
Wonder what that's all about?

COLORBLIND

We're not white.
We're not black.
Or red or tan.

Forget hazel,
Green, blue,
And brown.

Red hair, auburn,
Brunette or blonde.

Colors don't mean a damned thing.

Let's go blind for just one day,
What will our hearts and minds say?
Maybe our blindness will make us see.
Inside we're the same. The you's and the me's.

DREAMS

Out to play I slam the door.
Memories of years before.

Proof of life without a screen,
Lies in pictures old as dreams.

What I'd give for one more run,
Bareback horse into the sun.

Getting lost in forest thick,
No one worried, no one sick.

Of hearing news no telling lies,
No murder where a family dies.

Oh, how I wish for days long gone,
When every day was like a song.

When families sat at dinnertime,
To talk and share each day in kind.

For now, my memories must due.
Too bad our young will have no clue.

It's sad they'll miss in living life,
Of years gone by like mine.

THE WRONG STUFF

I'm so brittle, I break before glass.
Then reach for anything that stops the pain.
So soft…so weak…so broken and sad.
And disillusioned.

I think it all started way back, when I got those trophies.

For losing.

QUESTIONS?

Where'd the me-too movement go?
We're supposed to be pro-woman, I know.
So now, we hate all white men?
Are illegals legal? Or is honesty a sin?
Then there's Americans, you and your kin,
Devalued daily, stripped of sovereign.
Why do we lose if we try hard to win?
Just more questions, never to end.

Whatever they're doing they refuse to change.
I guess it's now…the land of the strange.

EMILY POST

Let's make a law that breaks a law.
Ignore the common payola flaw.
Or,
Should we ask Emily Post?

Cause disease among our own.
Give away our happy home.
Or,
Should we ask Emily Post?

Punish those who try do good.
Praise the hate of brotherhood.
Or,
Should we ask Emily Post?

Yes, oh yes!
Let's poke the ghost!
Speak to us now, dear Emily Post!

A NATION'S HOPE

A nation of haters?
Desolaters?
What we've become,
Deaf, blind, and dumb?

Wind always brings change,
But nothing as strange,
Fully deranged,
With no sense of shame.

Promises ditched,
Yes and no switched,
The pitch turned a bitch.
Now what do we do?

Turn from the hate,
Open the gate.
It's never too late,
To set things straight.

Remember what's right,
And good common sense,
Let's move from today,
And make it past-tense.

THE GREAT LOSS

Perspective,
Respect,
Ethics,
Healthy debate,
Common sense...
Essential attributes gone extinct in this,
Our wounded world.

THE TEN

Solve the world's problems.
Everyone has a point of view.
I sit in a green room by an orange roaring fire,
And ponder.

I'm not arrogant but if you were to ask me,
This is what I'd say:

Keep your sanity, weigh work, and play.
Don't kill to kill, value the day.

Respect for your parents, family, and friends,
Discord will happen, so make your amends.

When they become tempting, turn upside-down up,
Don't give to the thrill, tend your own cup.

Practice in truth, curb your desires,
Care for your loved ones, turn from the liars.

Remember, in death, you can't take possessions,
But one that will follow, will be your transgressions.

Live for the love of what you believe,
Example of mind, what you do, say and see.

Now that I've finished I seek no applaud,
They're already written, by no other than God.

SCIENCE

Follow the science, as good neighbors die,
Healing orders elude doctor's eyes.

Follow the science, between our loins,
Some claim we're more than girls or boys.

Follow the science, the powerful high,
Don't contradict, don't question, comply.

Follow the science, but data tells,
A different truth, their numbers don't jell.

Follow the science, it changes each day,
Hidden in money, its true pathway.

I'd follow the science if only I could,
But damn, I can't find it, guess I'm screwed.

THE BIG FAULT

Some live with good intentions,
Some live with bad intentions.

But one thing dear,
This past year…it's a telling, telling lesson.

One big fault I have found,
Don't put your faith in humans.

BLASPHEME*

Religion.
The unspeakable.
Except when it's that last option in your crafty toolbox,
To get what you want.

*written for the hypocritical manipulator of their own false gods

WEBSTER-WOKE PART 1

Bad used to mean: terrible.
Normal used to mean: typical or expected.
Binary used to mean: 01.

Gender used to mean: sex, male or female, of a human.
Racism used to mean: prejudice against another.
Lockdown used to mean: confining criminals to their cells.

Criminal used to mean: lawbreaker.
Victim used to mean: a person injured or killed by another.
Woke used to mean: the past tense of wake.

Cancel used to mean: vacate an event.
Freedom used to mean: the right to act, speak,
or think as desired within the boundaries of the law.

Immunity used to mean…well…

You get it.

WEBSTER-WOKE PART 2

Can't laugh, don't smile.
Don't say that word.
Its meaning different,
When last you heard.

Walk on eggs,
And if you slip,
Fake a sneeze and,
Follow that tip.

It's hard work to talk,
Both friend and foe,
The words you speak,
The less you know.

Expand The Book,
Five hundred and more,
It changes each day,
To make my head sore.

WORTH REPEATING

Lies are true.
Lies are true.
Lies are true.
Lies are true.
Lies are true.
Lies are true.
Lies are true.
Lies are true.
Lies are true.
Lies are true.
Lies are true.
Lies are true.
Lies are true.
Lies are true.
Lies are true.
Lies are true.
Lies are true.
Lies are true.
Lies are true.
Lies are true.
Lies are true.

No matter how many times they say it,
Doesn't make it so.

THE EVENING NOOSE

I'm like most. I listen every night. Just the facts ma'am.
I admit, my expectations are stuck in the '70s.

Each day I hope they'll change their approach.
The only true segment's the performing cockroach.

Everything else is what if, why not?
Opinions from one commercial to another,
But no chance to offer mine.

News is not news, just commentary.
Flip the channels, you hear the contrary.

Take it all in and decide what you think.
Just flip a coin or pick a straw.
One says it's true.
The other says lie.

Maybe I should turn it off.
Promise me, they'll be no loss,
Of head nor heart nor silent nights,
With time I feel familiar sights,
Of smiles and laughter,
Talks ever after…

Living sure is fun.

HELP WANTED

"We have to pass the bill,
so we can find out what's in it…
Our (multi-trillion dollar) spending
bill will cost nothing. Nothing." [1]

"Now that's what I call back-asswards.
Insanity.
Ignorant.
Lacking logic, common sense,
And intelligence.
The super-deluxe version of stupidity." [2]

[1] Nancy Pelosi, speaker of the house of the United States of America
[2] Marilyn Minette, author

76

THE WAR WITHIN

No rounds of rounds need be dropped here,
Eyes roll all up, they think we're queer,
They see and watch our great divide,
Of cracks that swallow what we can't hide.
They conquer me, we conquer you.
The great replace, no room for two.

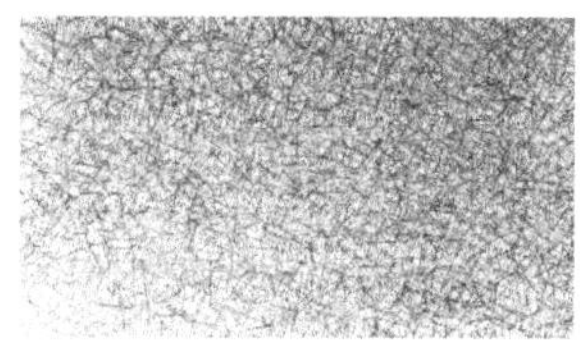

THE CHOSEN ONE

"Politic" a dirty word.
Wash your mouth if it is heard.
Nonsense spills of thoughts absurd,
Fill the ears with soured curd.

If you go there, sorry be,
Parasites await to feed,
Crawl the holes of dark to see,
Illusion light the real ugly.

On second thought if you can stand,
We need another ethics man,
Among the caving slaving band,
Of crazy those who hate this land.

So if you feel and if you still,
Want, I'll send you off to kill,
The hate, the malice, evil filled,
In grandiose of justice ill.

Good luck my son, God speed your way,
Spend well your time with each new day,
Do the right, resist the nay,
Our land has chosen you today.

78

THE FEW

A small group of loud voices,
Can change everything.

Sometimes for the good.
But not always.

STRAIGHT UP

Blow me to Egypt the dry sand blows.
Take a dehumidifier, Heaven knows.
Don't judge books by covers, lover.
Let's just ban 'em instead.

Have a heart when you hear the news,
Don't listen close, it gives you the blues.
Exercise daily, diet right,
Start tomorrow, feast tonight.

Misery loves company,
You, them, me.
Your job's not important,
They simply refuse to see.

They make the rules,
Then fail to buy,
Perhaps they want us,
Just to die.

They hear me sneeze,
Say God bless me,
Words don't make it,
You son-of-a-bully.

Their measured jargon cries tear gas. 
Let 'em shove themselves up their own ass.

FRIDAY'S FRIDAY

Day's been hard.
But one thing I still do.
Time to party like before.
Even if it's in my head.

Let's pile our hair and paint our lips.
You drive. I'll route you right.
The way to Fridays on Friday night.
Just something we used to do.

Smooth shuffle round the bar,
Feel all eyes follow far.
Hands here and here and there and there.
Just something we used to do.

Smile meets smile.
We take free wine as pass we by.
Let's do it again, and one more time.
Just something we used to do.

PARTIES

Those dreaded political parties.
Democrats, Independents, and Republicans.
(In alphabetical order, you note.
No favoritism here.)

I'm not among one pedigree.
Some of this and a little of that,
I'm hybrid mixed as you can see.
I claim no blinded piety.

My will is free, a mind of mine.
When asked I'll tell, perhaps in rhyme.
I think alone, consider time.
And always free to change of mind.

I tell myself to think for me,
And not for fads, what's on TV.
I tap my conscience, what's right, what's wrong,
Follow my heart and pray for strong.

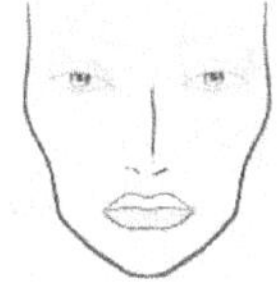

CANCEL MUCH?

Cancel Culture's not civilized,
It's made our history un-legitimized,
As most sit back immobilized,
While few shout loud demoralize!

They claim they are the civilized,
Take a life and criticize,
Don't they know you saved their lives,
Yesterday with the traumatized?

Love to make you destabilized,
They hate the word…harmonize,
Go overboard with penalize,
As they become desensitized.

Now our language demonized,
How much more can be scrutinized?
Who are they to moralize?
Paralyze?
Scandalize?
Brutalize?
And dehumanize?

Recognize,
And realize.
Cease the judgment rush!
Oh, one more thing…
Cancel much?

ISN'T IT?

Go shoplift something you want,
Not a problem.
Police are ordered to stand down.
It's okay.
Isn't it?

Kick that old man down the street,
Not a problem.
And if you missed it, it'll be posted soon,
Give them a minute.
No big deal.
It's okay.
Isn't it?

Plow down that business,
Not a problem.
Anyhow, they've been through it before.
All is well.
Isn't it?

Burn the streets, throw the pipe bombs,
Shoot a few rounds in the air or the crowd.
Not a problem.
After all, it's a peaceful protest.
Isn't it?

Well, isn't it?

TOGETHER

A new attitude,
Of what we once knew.
Not all was perfect,
But not all was flawed.

God help us,
We're only human,
But we can make our wrongs right.
Find our way through the night.

We need each other to win this war,
To meet head-on,
Against evil and unjust.
We once again must find trust.

Come together. Set aside.
Forgive the hate. Find the love.
We can make it happen.
United.
We can stand again.

WORDS

I hope you're mad, or glad, or sad.
I hope I've stirred emotion.
Maybe even lit a fire,
Words are like a potion.

Claim your truth with bold compassion,
Don't tear down - build with passion,
Overflow your heart and sing,
Live a life worth everything.

THE BEGINNING

So here we are, an end of ends.
A book of poems someone has penned.
But bigger than a few mixed words,
Is how humanity is served.

Lose respect, degrade a friend,
Is the beginning of our end.
Not just humanity, you see,
It's the great dehumanization of you and me.

Wake up and see,
Don't let it be…
The end of you,
The end of me.

Hope remains eternal.

DOWNSIDE UP

ABOUT THE AUTHOR

Marilyn Minette grew up in the beautiful midwest countryside with her mother, father, brother, and little dog. Void of a real childhood, her love of music and dance consumed her life. By age fourteen, Marilyn had sixteen private piano and vocal students. She holds a BE degree and enjoys writing music and poetry.

A former manager of a select teaching facility, Marilyn now devotes her time to her creative side.

Musician turned author, Marilyn's writing style is one of truth, hope, and forgiveness. *Downside Up* is an emotional reflection of the frustration during these covid times.

Marilyn's love of art, prose, and poetry is beautifully displayed in her various works. Visit Amazon.com to see additional books by this author, including numerous prose and poetry collections as well as her novel in trilogy form.

Check out Marilyn's website here:
www.marilynminettebooks.com

Follow her on Instagram:
@marilyn_minette

www.ingramcontent.com/pod-product-compliance
Lightning Source LLC
Chambersburg PA
CBHW061024250726
48659CB00019B/447